Kwanzaa Year Round

KWANZAA
ANNUAL FAMILY BOOK
for

The _____ Family

Year_____

Address

_____
_____
_____
_____

By Regina G. Ray

KWANZAA
ANNUAL FAMILY BOOK
Copyright © May 2022

Regina G. Ray

ALL RIGHTS RESERVED

No portion of this publication may be reproduce, stored in any electronic system, or transmitted in any form or by any means, electronic, mechanical, photocopy, recording, or otherwise, without written permission from the author. Brief quotations may be used in literary reviews.

Cover: by Regina. G. Ray

First printing: May 2022
Available through amazon.com

ISBN: 978-1-7365935-2-3

Also purchase at amazon.com: Contemplations In Black
ISBN: 978-1-736935-0-9
and
Balance In Black
ISBN: 978-1-7365935-1-6

Kwanzaa Year Round
Annual Family Book

Family Griots: _____

_____

_____

A Griot is a West African storyteller. Griots are responsible for maintaining the oral family stories and traditions. They keep records of all the births, deaths, and marriages through the generations of the village or family.

Griots originated in the 13th century in the Mande Empire of Mali. For centuries they have told and retold the stories of the empire, keeping their stories and traditions alive. [excerpt from Seckou Keita, admin@seckoumusic.com, 2019]

FAMILY MEMBER LIST

- Name:_____
  D.O.B. or Age:_____
- Name:_____
  D.O.B. or Age:_____
- Name:_____
  D.O.B. or Age:_____
- Name:_____
  D.O.B. or Age:_____
- Name:_____
  D.O.B. or Age:_____
- Name:_____
  D.O.B. or Age:_____
- Name:_____
  D.O.B. or Age:_____
- Name:_____
  D.O.B. or Age:_____
- Name:_____
  D.O.B. or Age:_____

- ❖ Name:_____
   D.O.B. or Age:_____
- ❖ Name:_____
   D.O.B. or Age:_____
- ❖ Name:_____
   D.O.B. or Age:_____
- ❖ Name:_____
   D.O.B. or Age:_____
- ❖ Name:_____
   D.O.B. or Age:_____
- ❖ Name:_____
   D.O.B. or Age:_____
- ❖ Name:_____
   D.O.B. or Age:_____
- ❖ Name:_____
   D.O.B. or Age:_____
- ❖ Name:_____
   D.O.B. or Age:_____
- ❖ Name:_____
   D.O.B. or Age:_____
- ❖ Name:_____
   D.O.B. or Age:_____

New Births	Marriages	Deaths
_____	_____	_____
_____	_____	_____
_____	_____	_____

What Is Kwanzaa?

By Regina G. Ray

Kwanzaa is not a faith or a religion. Kwanzaa is a cultural celebration for those who recognize, and acknowledge the celebration of their African ancestry. This cultural event attempts to mend that which was torn apart in the Diaspora and the resultant African American communities. It is a time of commemoration, remembrance, and honor from those living to the Creator and to those who are our Ancestors; those who are our foremothers and forefathers who sacrificed during difficult past times, that we as their descendants may live a better life today.

Kwanzaa provides the beneficial option for participation in an African cultural celebration during the holiday season. It serves to return our focus internally as a community, away from commercial losses and practices that do not benefit the long term well being of African peoples. Kwanzaa too is an educational opportunity for our youth to learn traditional practices that honor their Elders, Ancestors, and Self.

Kwanzaa provides a family setting for us to tell our family stories according to our own written and oral tellings. Kwanzaa is a time for reflection and recognition of each family member's annual accomplishments and contributions that make our lives better today. We must develop a spirit of 'expectations' for the family and celebrate its fulfillment. Let us appreciate the talents and strengths of one another; then look forward to the coming year.

Read aloud the Principles of Kwanzaa and discuss how each can be incorporated into our daily lives. Refer to the 'Kwanzaa Year Round Solar Calendar' and have a Happy Kwanzaa!

Kwanzaa Year Round

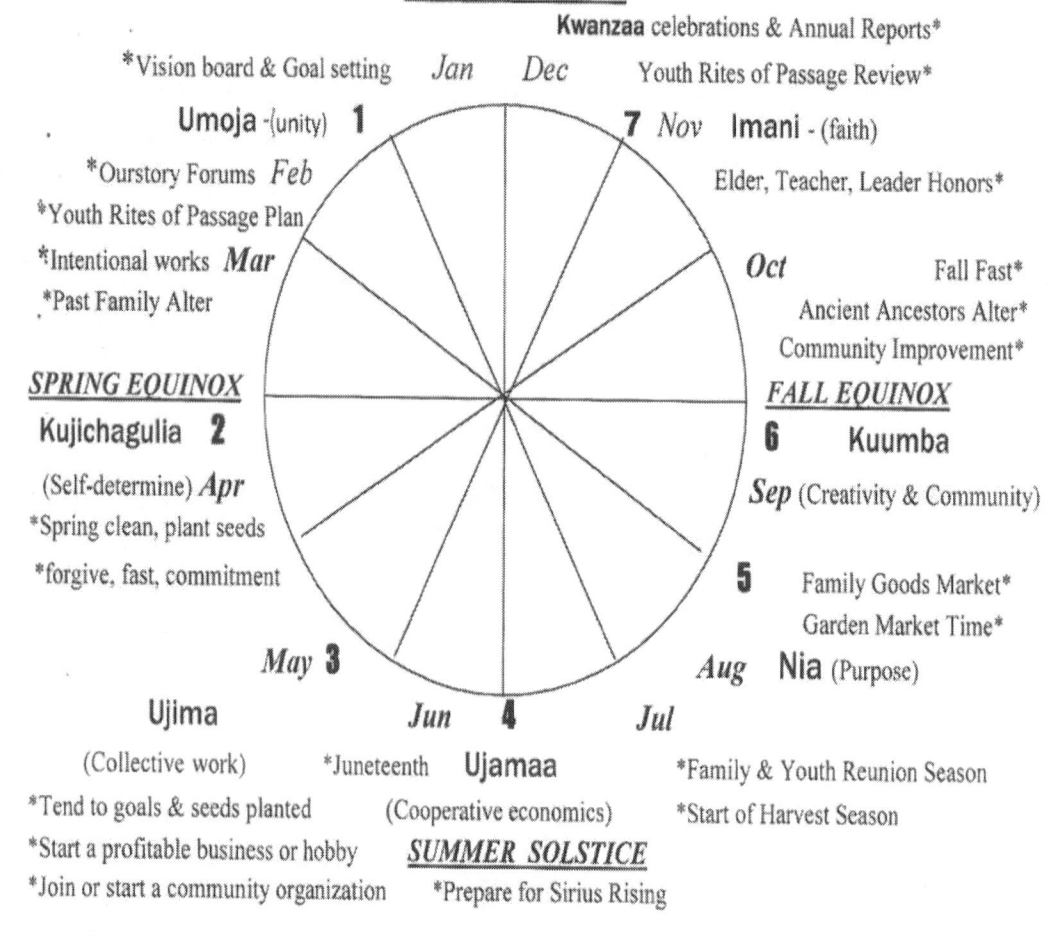

WINTER SOLSTICE

Kwanzaa celebrations & Annual Reports*

*Vision board & Goal setting   *Jan*   *Dec*   Youth Rites of Passage Review*

Umoja -(unity) **1**   **7** *Nov*   **Imani** - (faith)

*Ourstory Forums *Feb*

Youth Rites of Passage Plan   Elder, Teacher, Leader Honors

*Intentional works *Mar*   *Oct*   Fall Fast*

Past Family Alter   Ancient Ancestors Alter

Community Improvement*

SPRING EQUINOX   FALL EQUINOX

Kujichagulia **2**   **6**   **Kuumba**

(Self-determine) *Apr*   *Sep* (Creativity & Community)

*Spring clean, plant seeds

*forgive, fast, commitment   **5**   Family Goods Market*

Garden Market Time*

May **3**   *Aug*   **Nia** (Purpose)

Ujima   *Jun*   **4**   *Jul*

(Collective work)   *Juneteenth   **Ujamaa**   *Family & Youth Reunion Season

*Tend to goals & seeds planted   (Cooperative economics)   *Start of Harvest Season

*Start a profitable business or hobby   **SUMMER SOLSTICE**

*Join or start a community organization   *Prepare for Sirius Rising

Kwanzaa Year Round

By Regina G. Ray

December 26 – Jan 1 brings into focus Kwanzaa Celebration;
Kwanzaa was the brain-child of Dr. Maulana Karenga, professor and chairman of African Studies at California State University, created 1966 to bring African Americans together as a community. There are seven guiding Principles of Kwanzaa that represent seven values of African culture that help build and reinforce community. First created as a week-long observance, Kwanzaa is now recognized 'Year Round', culminating in an end- of- year annual celebration. Family, friends, and children are all encouraged to participate in the 'Kwanzaa Year Round Calendar' that has been designed to keep everyone on track to learn, prosper, and live well.

During the winter solstice Kwanzaa Celebration, we observe each Principle of Kwanzaa to give and affirm an 'Annual Accounting' of the past year's achievements. These achievements are to be recorded in an annual report. Accounted for in the report shall be each living family member's achievements and contributions, and an acknowledgement of new births and of those family members who have passed-on during the course of that year. Host a Kwanzaa gathering, share the family story, read a story aloud, play games of fun, and make homemade gifts to share.

Jan. 1 begins the New Calendar Year

Jan. 1 – Jan. 31 is a great time for personal meditations and reflections of family.
- ❖ This is the time to make plans for self improvement and goals for the coming year. Record and hang them as a daily reminder. Read and recite *Tree of Life* affirmations aloud to acknowledge and dedicate yourself to your highest consciousness.

Feb. 1 – March 14 brings into focus the Kwanzaa Principle
Umoja – Unity;
to strive for and maintain unity in the family, community, nation, and race.

- ❖ Nationally known as Black History Month, spend time together with family and friends in pursuit of black historical facts and knowledge. Read books, watch documentaries, and attend lectures to improve upon knowledge of 'Our Story.'
- ❖ Youth Rites of Passage Planning.
  Assess the annual needs for each youth in the family and make plans to fulfill them. Review the plans with the family and youth for feedback and suggestions.

March 15 – April 14 brings into focus the Kwanzaa Principle
> ***Kujichagulia*** *– Self Determination;*
> *to define ourselves, name ourselves, create for ourselves, and speak for ourselves.*

- ❖ Now is the time to set into motion all goals and plans for improvement. Step out of your comfort zone to put into motion plans toward your annual goals.
- ❖ Clean out physically and spiritually to clear a path for success.
- ❖ Plant new seeds to get an early start in your garden.
- ❖ Refresh and redecorate the 'Family' alter. Allow the youth to assist while telling stories of remembrance. Visit ancestral grave sites to lay flowers if desired.

April 15 – June 15 brings into focus the Kwanzaa Principle
> ***Ujima*** *– Collective Work and Responsibility;*
> *to build and maintain our community together and make our brothers' and sisters' problems our problems and solve them together.*

- ❖ This is a good time for one-on-one and group counseling together to develop a meeting of the minds and proceed on one accord. The whole family will benefit from Ujima. Work together on a community project to spread the love.
- ❖ Fasting mid April for 10 or more days will bring clarity to mind and spirit.
- ❖ A great time for wedding vows; Plan in advance for multiple couples to share vows in a 'mass ceremony.'

June 15 – July 31 brings into focus the Kwanzaa Principle
> ***Ujamaa*** *– Cooperative Economics;*
> *to build and maintain our own gardens, stores, shops and other businesses and to profit from them together.*

If you have started Umoja, Kujichagulia, and Ujima then you have gotten a great start to the year. Your house, temple, and spirit have been through a cleanse. The goals and seeds that you planted have taken root, and you are empowered by your honors to the Ancestors.

- ❖ Continue to plant seeds in your garden for a summer and fall crop.
- ❖ Prepare for the helical rising of the Sirius Star. Host a 'Star Gazing' gathering to watch the annual event with others. Read aloud the stories of cosmic beginnings; [Ref; see *Contemplations In Black*]

August 1 – Sep. 15 brings into focus the Kwanzaa Principle
Nia – Purpose;
to make our collective vocation the building and developing of our community in order to restore our people to our traditional greatness.

- ❖ This is the season of immediate and extended 'Family Reunions'; home cooking, children meeting their cousins, aunties, and uncles; honoring our Grandparents and elders.
- ❖ Harvest time; harvest of the fruits of our labor begins. Share home grown veggies and fruits with family, neighbors and friends.

September 15 – October 31 brings into focus the Kwanzaa Principle
Kuumba – Creativity and Community Improvement;
to do always all that we can, in order to leave our community more beautiful and beneficial than we inherited it.

- ❖ 'Annual Market Time' is a time to show-off the products of our gifts and talents. This is a great time for financial harvest. Sell your fruits, products, and gifts in the market square.
- ❖ Fall fasting; a short fast for cleansing and for 'Ancient Ancestral' remembrance and honoring. Take the time to make or refresh your 'Ancient Ancestral' alter during mid-October for the coming Day of the Spirits.

Nov. 1 – Dec. 24 brings into focus the Kwanzaa Principle
Imani – Faith;
to believe with all our heart in our people, our parents, our teachers, our leaders, and the righteousness and victory of our elevation.

- ❖ As we have encouraged the participation of the youth in Kwanzaa activities throughout the year, this is a special time to review that their Rites of Passage have been acknowledged, supported, and fulfilled by the family, beginning with the parents and throughout – without fail. We each must step up and assure that each child's needs are met physically, financially, and spiritually; "We each have an obligation to make available to our children the love, care, and security required for a healthy mind, body, and spirit.

    Protect the wellbeing of every boy and girl. Smile upon them, share your time, speak a positive word, encourage them to read and learn their story. These things will build health and strength to our community for a better future for all." [Ref; Contemplations In Black]

- ❖ Self-Examination is encouraged year round by the posting and daily reciting of the 'Laws of Maat' and to reconcile all injustices for as much as possible. This is the time to reflect upon the year and make right any wrongs which you bare responsibility, prior to entering the Kwanzaa Celebration season.

    "The flail serves as a reminder that daily judgment comes from within, in preparation for that faithful day when life before the 'Council of Elders' judge what un-reconciled remains."

    [Ref; Contemplations In Black]

December 25 – January 1

is the beginning of the **Kwanzaa Celebration Week**. Follow the Kwanzaa program as introduced by its founder Dr. Maulana Karenga.

- ❖ Present the Family Annual Report. Give an accounting of all family. Recognize each family member and their annual accomplishments.

Kwanzaa Celebration

[https://www.interexchange.org/articles/career-training-usa/history-principles-and-symbols-of-kwanzaa/]

The holiday is relatively new, compared to other holidays celebrated in the U.S. Dr. Maulana Karenga, professor and chairman of Africana Studies at California State University first created Kwanzaa in 1966. He created this to bring African-Americans together as a community. Dr. Karenga created seven guiding principles to be discussed during the week of Kwanzaa. The seven principles represent seven values of African culture that help build and reinforce community among African-Americans. Each day a different principle is discussed, and each day a candle is lit on the kinara (candleholder). On the first night, the center Black candle is lit, and the principle of umoja, or unity is discussed. On the final day of Kwanzaa, families enjoy an African feast, called karamu. The language of Kwanzaa is Swahili.

Habari Gani !!! (Kwanzaa greeting)

Kwanzaa has seven core principles, or NguzoSaba:

1. Umoja: Unity
To strive for and maintain unity in the family, community, nation, and race.

2. Kujichagulia: Self-Determination:
To define ourselves, name ourselves, create for ourselves, and speak for ourselves.

3. Ujima: Collective Work and Responsibility
To build and maintain our community together and make our brothers' and sisters' problems our problems and solve them together.

4. Ujamaa: Cooperative Economics
To build and maintain our own stores, shops, and other businesses and to profit from them together.

5. Nia: Purpose
To make our collective vocation the building and developing of our community in order to restore our people to their traditional greatness.

6. Kuumba: Creativity
To do always as much as we can, in the way we can, in order to leave our community more beautiful and beneficial than we inherited it.

7. Imani: Faith
To believe with all our heart in our people, our parents, our teachers, our leaders, and the righteousness and victory of our struggle.

Kwanzaa Celebration Checklist

_____ : The Mat; Mkeka (*m-KAY-kah*): A mat woven of fabric, raffia, or even paper. The Mkeka is important because the other holiday implements rest upon it. Symbolizes the experiences, culture, achievements and sacrifices of our ancestors upon which our lives are built.

_____ The Unity Cup; Kikombe cha Umoja (*kee-KOHM-bay cha oo-MOH-jah*): Representing family and community unity. When the Unity cup filled with water, juice, or wine, a little bit is poured out as reminder and respect for our ancestors. The cup is then passed around and shared with those gathered, with each person taking a sip.

_____ The Crops; Mazao (*mah-AH-oh*): The fruits and vegetables that are the result of the harvest. Bananas, mangoes, peaches, plantains, oranges, or whatever might be the family favorites. The Mazao are placed on the Mkeka and are shared and eaten to honor the work of the people it took to grow them.

_____ **The Candleholder; Kinara** (*kee-NAH-rah*): Representing our African ancestors, the Kinara holds the seven candles that symbolize the Nguzo Saba. The Kinara is placed on the Mkeka and holds the Mishumaa Saba (the seven candles).

_____ **The Seven Candles Mishumaa Saba** (*mee-shoo-MAH SAH-ba*): Seven candles, representing the seven principles of Nguzo Saba, which are placed in the Kwanzaa Kinara. The colors of the candles are red, green, and Black which are the colors of the Bendera (or Pan-African Flag).

_____ **The Corn Muhindi** (*moo-HEEN-dee*): Represents the children (and future) of the family. One suke (ear) of corn is placed on the Mkeka for each child in the family. If there are no children in the family one suke is still placed on the Mkeka to symbolize the children of the community.

The Muhindi also represents the Native Americans who were the first inhabitants of the land. Without whom there would be no corn, also known as Maize. It is used as acknowledgment and respect of their contribution to the culture and ancestors of the African American.
Note: A single ear of corn can also be known as Vibunzi. Indian Corn is sometimes used.

_____ **Gifts Zawadi** (*zah-WAH-dee*): Kwanzaa gifts given to children that will make them better people. The gifts should always include a book, video, or other educational item that will educate and inform the child. There should also be a gift know as a "heritage symbol". Something to remind the child of glory of the past and the promise of the future.

You, your family and your community can use great creativity in the observance of Kwanzaa. The area in your home where you set up the Kwanzaa altar or table can be decorated in the same spirit as other holidays. Create posters and banners to hang on the walls, add African sculptures or other artwork to the display. Many crafts and decorations can be created by the children of the home to be used in your Kwanzaa display.

Village Gathering Ceremony
Kwanzaa Celebration;
first; as in "first fruits of the harvest"

Greetings
Habari Gani ; Swahili for 'What's the news?!'
Exercise #1 - Repeat after me: "Habari Gani"
This is the greeting of Kwanzaa
Exercise #2 – Greet the person on each side of you with "Habari Gani"
Response – say a Kwanzaa principle such as "Umoja"
Extra: (Responses: Habari yako – I'm doing well)
Nzuri – beautiful, good, nice, fine

Libations

Tools needed: Water
                             Libation vessel (to catch water)
                             Libation cup (to pour water)

"We ask the Creator and Ancestors to continue to watch over and guide us through the unknowns of this life on earth and to the afterlife."

We pour libations: "in honor of the Creator and the Creation."

We pour libations: " in remembrance of our Ancient Ancestors."
(List names of Ancient Ancestors to call upon)

We pour libations: as "We remember the names of our loved ones who have gone on before us;
- Fathers and Fathers of our Fathers and all of their family members,
- Mothers and Mothers of our Mothers and all of their family members,
- Sisters, Brothers, Children and loved ones"

We pour libations: "to our ancestors known & unknown"
                           "We pour libations to remember thee."

Recognitions

Youngest:
Exercise #3   Recognize the youngest attendee

Elders and Ancestors: Occupy a high place in African culture
Exercise #4   Everyone raise a hand.
                         Lower your hand if you are under 20
                         Lower your hand if you are under 30
                         Lower your hand if you are under 50
                         Lower your hand if you are under 70
                         Lower your hand if you are under 80
                         Lower your hand if you are under 90

Exercise #5   Top 3 elders recognized with name, age and comments.

Lessons

Exercise #6

Read aloud: *'A Kwanzaa Story'* – see Kwanzaa instructions

Read aloud: Introduction to the Ceremony Table – see Kwanzaa Celebration Checklist

Read aloud: The principles of Kwanzaa – see the NguzoSaba list

Read aloud: The Family Annual Kwanzaa Report

Extended Ceremony (cont'd)

Feast of First Fruits (Karamu Kwanzaa)
Kwanzaa can be shared with a great feast served.

Creativity (Kuumba)
Home-made gifts (za-wah'-dee) are shared or prepared by the children to share.

Games & Fun

Exercise #7
Story telling is a big part of African culture; an enlightening form of entertainment and sharing. Read *A Kwanzaa Story* aloud.

A Kwanzaa Story
"In the beginning of time, the earth's lands were one. This is found in the science of Plate Tectonics. During that time there lived the first woman and man who walked the earth. As this woman and man multiplied, their dwellings spread out across the land from one end of the earth to the other end until the land began to rock, shake, and drift apart.

The gathered waters began to spill between the cracks. There was a time when one could stand with their feet straddled on two separate lands with a river running between. But soon the waters spilled so widely that man had to swim to get from one side to the other.

As waters rose, and the lands drifted further apart, each person remained on their respective lands. Eventually a boat was required to reach distant shores. This is why even today we can find this first man on every continent around the world."

Exercise #8
Gathering in a circle (umoja) is an important practice in African culture. We gather around to eat, sing, dance, and play games.

Play a color seeking game of 'I Spy.' Spy out an object and say aloud "I spy something (color of object)" Each participant takes a turn guessing what the object is. Whoever guesses correctly takes the next turn until everyone gets a turn or tires of the game.

Exercise #9
Sing a song together
Make a dance circle as dancers take turns at the center.

Farewell

Look forward to new days ahead.
> *Kwa heri* / **kwa herini** (more than one person) - good-bye
> *Tutaonana* - see you later
> *Nafurahi kukuona* - nice to meet you
> *Lala salama* - goodnight

Family Member Record:_____

Annual Goals
_____
_____
_____
_____
_____
_____

Accomplishments_____
_____
_____
_____
_____
_____
_____
_____
_____
_____
_____
_____
_____
_____
_____
_____

Family Member Record:_____

Annual Goals
_____
_____
_____
_____
_____
_____

Accomplishments_____
_____
_____
_____
_____
_____
_____
_____
_____
_____
_____
_____
_____
_____
_____
_____

Family Member Record:_____

Annual Goals
_____
_____
_____
_____
_____
_____

Accomplishments_____
_____
_____
_____
_____
_____
_____
_____
_____
_____
_____
_____
_____
_____

Family Member Record:_____

Annual Goals
_____
_____
_____
_____
_____

Accomplishments_____
_____
_____
_____
_____
_____
_____
_____
_____
_____
_____
_____
_____

Family Member Record:_____

Annual Goals

_____
_____
_____
_____
_____
_____

Accomplishments_____

_____
_____
_____
_____
_____
_____
_____
_____
_____
_____
_____
_____
_____

Family Member Record: _____

Annual Goals
_____
_____
_____
_____
_____
_____

Accomplishments_____
_____
_____
_____
_____
_____
_____
_____
_____
_____
_____
_____
_____
_____
_____

Family Member Record:_____

Annual Goals
_____
_____
_____
_____
_____
_____

Accomplishments_____
_____
_____
_____
_____
_____
_____
_____
_____
_____
_____
_____
_____
_____
_____
_____
_____

Family Member Record:_____

Annual Goals
_____
_____
_____
_____
_____
_____

Accomplishments_____
_____
_____
_____
_____
_____
_____
_____
_____
_____
_____
_____
_____
_____
_____

Family Member Record:_____

Annual Goals
_____
_____
_____
_____
_____
_____

Accomplishments_____
_____
_____
_____
_____
_____
_____
_____
_____
_____
_____
_____
_____
_____
_____
_____
_____

Family Member Record:_____

Annual Goals
_____
_____
_____
_____
_____
_____
_____

Accomplishments_____
_____
_____
_____
_____
_____
_____
_____
_____
_____
_____
_____
_____
_____
_____
_____
_____

Family Member Record: _____

Annual Goals

_____
_____
_____
_____
_____
_____

Accomplishments_____

_____
_____
_____
_____
_____
_____
_____
_____
_____
_____
_____
_____
_____
_____
_____
_____

Family Member Record:_____

Annual Goals
_____
_____
_____
_____
_____
_____

Accomplishments_____
_____
_____
_____
_____
_____
_____
_____
_____
_____
_____
_____
_____
_____
_____

Family Member Record:_____

Annual Goals

_____
_____
_____
_____
_____
_____

Accomplishments_____

_____
_____
_____
_____
_____
_____
_____
_____
_____
_____
_____
_____
_____
_____
_____
_____

The Tree of Life

Sphere 1-6 are attributes of Higher Self

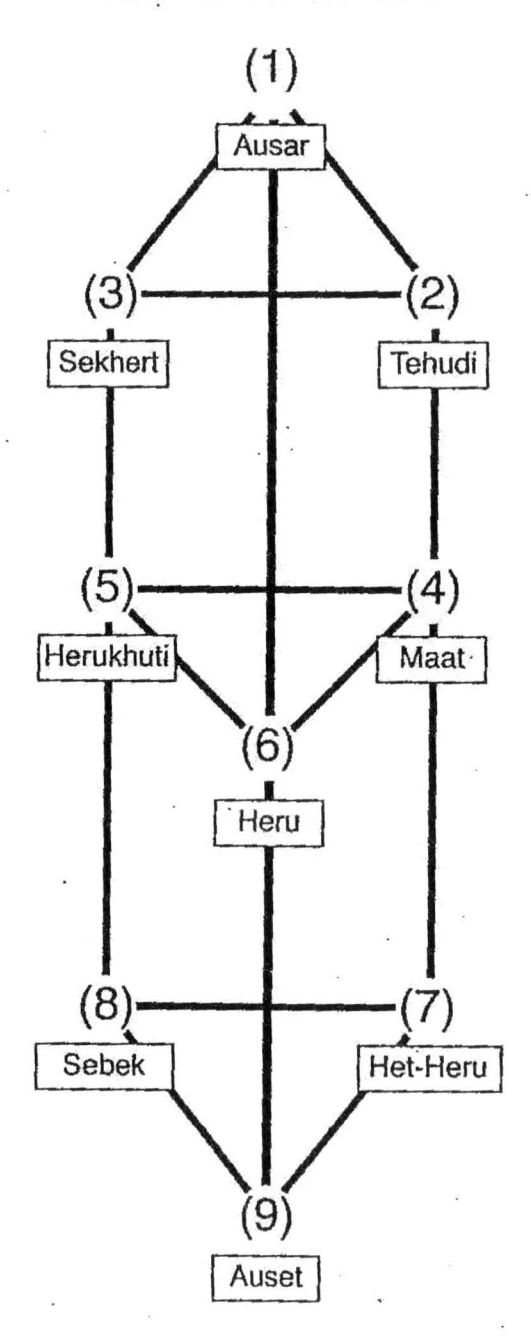

Sphere 7, 8 & 9 are active at birth

- (1) Ausar
- (2) Tehudi
- (3) Sekhert
- (4) Maat
- (5) Herukhuti
- (6) Heru
- (7) Het-Heru
- (8) Sebek
- (9) Auset

Ausar	Sphere 1 Divinity	Unity. The ability to be one with all things. The "Mummy", a nature so highly evolved, one is immune to all emotional or earthy influences.
Tehudi	Sphere 2 Divine Wisdom	The ability to intuit all knowledge, directly, first hand. "All knowing." The ability to communicate with each faculty of God directly. The level of the sage.
Sekhert	Sphere 3 Divine Power	Control of the life force, the formative base of all things in the world. Governs the cycles of life and death, yin and yang.
Maat	Sphere 4 Divine Truth	The ability to comprehend the natural law. Truth is a measure of how function adheres to form. Do we live according to God's design? The ability to acquire one's needs through an understanding of the laws governing a situation.
Herukhuti	Sphere 5 Justice	The attribute of defense and protection. The use of spiritual power to defend from external attack. The use of spiritual power to heal inside the body, internal attack.
Heru	Sphere 6 The Will	The ability to rise above fears and conditionings, and exercise the will. The use of the will to live truth. The ability to self regulate oneself.
Het Heru	Sphere 7 Harmony, Beauty	The ability to get along with people and things that are different from us. The full manifestation of the seductive aspect of our sexual nature. The ability to attract, physically and spiritually. The employment of the imagination to create.
Sebek	Sphere 8 Language	The faculty that allows us to separate and define the parts of a whole. Our ability to communicate thoughts, but not the act of thinking.
Auset	Sphere 9 Devotion	The faculty of trance. Devotion. The tendency to mimic others. The nurturing instinct.

The Tree of Life

Ancient wisdom can be found in the construct of a tree referred to as a '*mandala*.' Ancient texts reference two different trees;   1) *The Tree of Life*
2) *The Tree of Knowledge*

The Tree Of Life demonstrates the progression of man/woman through spiritual stages of development from birth. Within these ancient writings is a map of pre-recorded knowledge from those who have gone before. Their recorded awareness provides an overstanding of the generalizations of life for helpful navigation.

Starting from the bottom of the tree, (stages 9-7), it is recognized that every human is born with common faculties such as instinct, communication, socialization, and imagination. Additional faculties (stages 6-2) may be acquired through increased knowledge and divine awareness. It is beneficial to have an awareness of the faculties of the *Tree Of Life*. It is even more beneficial to learn how to navigate its ascension. Together with proper training and divine inspiration, it is possible for man/woman to reach his/her highest level of consciousness (stage 1). Study the stages listed here:

TREE OF LIFE AFFIRMATIONS:

9) Aset; Devotion (active at birth)

The faculty of trance; nurturing instinct; devotion; the tendency to mimic others.

> *I draw upon intuitive resources for the successful completion of plans and projects. I successfully cultivate talent and abilities with purpose and work. In thought, word, and deed I rest my life upon the Eternal Being. The Kingdom of Spirit is embodied in my flesh.*

❖

8) Sebek; Communication (active at birth)

The faculty that allows us to separate and define the parts of a whole; The ability to communicate thoughts, but not the act of thinking. Communication is one of the three faculties through which our behavior can be reprogrammed at will. Gain knowledge to grow beyond innate instincts. Prepare to make sacrifices for the spiritual awakening of the will and the life force.

I formulate and empower mental images of success with desires and emotions that motivate me to achieve.
I look forward with confidence to the perfect realization of eternal life.

❖

7) Het Heru; Harmony and Beauty (active at birth)

The ability to get along with people and things that are different; The full manifestation of a seductive and sexual nature; The ability to attract, physically and spiritually.

> *In all things, great and small, I see the beauty in divine expression. I do not yield to habits and negative behavior*
> *that bring pain and suffering.*

❖

6) Heru; The Will

Man's will; the freedom to choose is man's greatest gift from the Creator; the ability to rise above fears and conditionings and exercise the will; the use of the will to live in truth; the ability to self regulate oneself.

> *Instead of following the emotional compulsions of the human mind, I choose to joyfully activate the Creator's spiritual power within.*
> *Living from that will that is supported by unfailing wisdom and overstanding.*
> *Mine is a victorious life.*

❖

5) Herukhuti; Justice

The attribute of defense and protection. Our protection from the injustices of others can only come from our beings, the vessels of the Creator's wisdom and spiritual power in the world. This is your power to immediately cut the negative thoughts and emotions that obstruct good attributes from manifesting in your spirit; the use of spiritual power to defend from external attack; the use of spiritual power to heal inside the body from internal attacks.

> *I identify and transform the forces and conditions that attempt to obstruct my progress. I recognize the manifestation of the*
> *undeviating justice in all the circumstances of my life.*

4) Maat; Divine Truth

Because we are separated in the inferior part of our being, and united in the superior part, the emotion of unity which is love is the most powerful of all emotions. When we are able to radiate love as a spiritual force, it generates order, peace and harmony within our being and to others in our surroundings. Love is the key to peace and prosperity through cooperation and health; the ability to comprehend natural law. Truth is a measure of how function adheres to form; fidelity to an original standard based upon reality and actuality; the ability to acquire one's needs through an overstanding of the laws governing the situation.

> *I attract the resources that are required to facilitate my growth and development. From the exhaustless riches of limitless substance, I draw all things needful, both spiritual and material.*

3) Sekhert; Divine Power

The Creator provides everyone spiritual power in the absence of help or resources. Control of the life force is the formative base of all things in the world; it governs the cycles of life and death; yin and yang.

> *Filled with overstanding of its perfect law, I am guided moment by moment along the path of liberation. I perceive the vocation through which my unique energy pattern will find its highest expression.*

2) Tehuti; Divine Wisdom

The Creator has made it possible to intuit its word, that we may receive direct guidance in the affairs of our lives; the ability to intuit all knowledge directly, first hand; "All knowing;" the ability to communicate with each faculty of God directly; the level of Sage.

> *Through me its unfailing wisdom takes form in thought and word. I am fully aware of my innate talents and abilities.*

❖

1) Asar; Divinity

The spiritual center of our oneness with the Creator and the creation; absolute emotional impartiality is necessary for the realization of selflessness and transcendental peace; unity; the ability to be one with all things; the "mummy" state; a nature so highly evolved, one is immune to all emotional or earthly influences.

> *I am a center of expression for the primal will to do good which eternally creates and sustains the universe. All the power that ever was or will be is here now. I am a creative being with unlimited possibilities*

References

Karenga, Maulana. *Principles of Kwanzaa.* California State University. 1966. [https://www.interexchange.org/articles/career-training-usa/history-principles-and-symbols-of-kwanzaa/]

Keita, Seckou. admin@seckoumusic.com, 2019.

Morris, Yao Nyamekye. *The Return.* 2001.

Ray, Regina. *Contemplations In Black.* Amazon.com., December 2020.

Ray, Regina. *Balance In Black.* Amazon.com., May 2022.

Made in the USA
Middletown, DE
05 February 2025